# Yours Truly

I0161672

*Really this is yours.*

*Truly!*

M. Catherine Bunton

Llumina
PRESS

ISBN:  978-1-62550-402-9
        978-1-62550-261-2

# Acknowledgement

I would like to acknowledge the poetry of Emily Dickinson, both the influence it has had on the world at large and on me in particular. She literally set nature to music, and we all know how profoundly music affects us. My poetry can't compare, but it does have its own melody. It is meant to motivate. Teachers can "offer" it to their classes, not as an assignment, but as a gift, thus the chapters are called offerings. Since poetry can change the world, and ours is a world longing for its song to carry on, this book calls for a renaissance, a restoration of poetry's preeminence. One way to revive it is to give readers a chance to respond to it with immediacy and the passion of spontaneity. In the world of possibility, "a better place than prose," written responses can lead to ordinary insights that can change the world in extraordinary ways. Since there are so many more people today, a small to medium renaissance will do.

# Dedication

Some people accomplish certain things while others make it possible for them to do so. This book is dedicated to those who made my accomplishments possible.

*Were I to walk on crutches*
*One would be named*
*For my husband*
*Greg*
*And the other for my sister*
*Sue*
*~~~*
*Well actually I do*


*For*
*Your help*
*And love*
*And devotion*
*~~~*
*I forever thank both of you*

# Contents

# *Introduction*

poetry21.renaissance


Arrange words in a new way and
They can make a rhyme or a melody
They can be soothing to a culture and
Even revive a 20th Century verse

New arrangements composed of pure
Intentions and natural rhythms
Leave the old beat behind and
Explode into new personal poetries

Even Shakespeare could hear the cheer
Rising In the 21st Century air with

## *April's first-born flowers and all things rare*

While we commoners undeterred
Follow Emily Dickinson whose

### *Winds of Will are stirred*

~~~ And a new sound begins ~~~

It begins to fill the dark matter of space
With a common rhyme in lower case
And the prospect for Everyman to
Perhaps obtain sanctifying grace

# A Friendly Persuasion

I thought perhaps as a reader who chooses to respond to poetry, you might like the opportunity to create your own pen name, your own nom de plume so to speak.

Many writers throughout history used pen names like the now famous Nelle Harper Lee of *"To Kill a Mockingbird"* fame. She wrote as Harper Lee. J.K. Rowling wrote as Kenilworthy Whisp, and Steven King wrote as Richard Bachman.

There are many reasons to use a pen name. One reason is that's its fun. I offer you this occasion to see your own words on paper and listen to your own voice as you…Have Fun!

**This manuscript is authored by:**

_____

_____

# Offering I

## Discovering things about myself as I write

# Morning Rush

morning (môr′nĭng) the beginning or early period
rush (rŭsh) a sudden, brief exhilaration


I awake each morning in high spirits

with an anticipation of what challenge

the day might hold.  The anticipation

itself is a rush.


I rise thinking that I might grab on to a

passing inspiration and write something

to better the world.  It's good to dream.

Dreams are the morning clouds we

climb upon and fly into the day.

Today Let Your Thoughts Soar
The Days Are So Very Few
For You'll Remember The Days
You Tried Something New

I Offer A Sinatra Invitation To
"Come Fly With Me"
You'll Find Inside Yourself
Sweet Discovery

What do you Say?

_____

_____

_____

_____

_____

_____

_____

_____

_____

_____

_____

_____

_____

_____

_____

_____

# Crossing To Safety

Cut into threads
Like a cross stitch of life --
Time weaves its way
Through joy and strife

Shading the years
Like a starched widow's net
Holding the sun
Till it falls to its set

Her face through the net
Once seen in its prime
Now under the veil
Is crossed by time

Captured and set
In history's frame
It's no longer safe
From wrinkled shame

The threads of time
Alive like the moth
Quickly ravel
Clear through the cloth

The netting breaks
Its silken ties -- and
A Tinsel Rebellion
Starts round the eyes

Till the face neath the veil
Is a vanishing lie
And she's barely left
With time to die

# *Time Weaves Its Way*
## *Through My Life...*

# Now Dreams Are Magic Too

I was intimate with magic

My days were sheer delight

My nights were filled with stardust

Shining, Safe, and Bright


I played inside the yard

Watched by regal eyes

Being loved by a Queen

Was my enterprise


At two I knew of majesty

At six I learned the art

Of the Queen's beloved magic

I thought we'd never part


But nothing lasts

Or so it seems

Now magic days with Mom

Are locked inside my dreams

## *Dreams Make You Wonder*
## *What They're Really All About*

_____

_____

_____

_____

_____

_____

_____

_____

_____

_____

_____

_____

_____

_____

_____

_____

_____

_____

_____

_____

_____

_____

# Miss Fancy Free and Me

If I could catch a lightening bug
I'd put her on my thumb
She could be a lighthouse
Sending messages to "Come"

Then children everywhere
Could respond to her glow
Coming like playful dolphins
Swimming by to say hello

Then when she got sleepy
I would form a little bed
To rest her shining light
And lay her little head

Cradling her inside my palm
She'd sleep throughout the day
Protected safe and sound
Till the sun had gone away

I'd hold her tight till evening
When dusk comes creeping by
Then opening up my hand
I would set her out to fly

Tossing her into the air
She'd fly higher and higher
Once again she would be free
To set the night on fire

## *Am I Fancy Free?*

_____

_____

_____

_____

_____

_____

_____

_____

_____

_____

_____

_____

_____

_____

_____

_____

_____

_____

_____

_____

_____

_____

_____

_____

_____

_____

_____

_____

# Recycling Poetry

Can you tell that I have
Written this interactive book
With the hope that you will
Recycle my words into yours

~~~

Emily Dickinson is my favorite
Poet and I have tried to recycle
Some of her words into my own
She spent time engaging the
Children of Amherst by filling
Up a basket with cookies then
Lowering it down to them
From the window of her room

Then returning to her poetry
She would set out to create poems
That were as delightful and sweet
As the cookies she gave to the children
She recycled the world of nature
Into verses that captured it's spirit
Like this one,

"If I can stop one heart from breaking,
I shall not live in vain;
If I can ease one life the aching,
Or cool one pain,
Or help one fainting robin
Unto his nest again,
I shall not live in vain."

Emily Dickinson packed
Our whole reason for being
Into a wicker basket
She wrapped it tight and
Lowered it into our eternity

We practically inhale it
To feed our hungry
Famished heart with the
Sweet sugar of her poetry
Thus enriched we weave
A new nest of rhyme
To cool the pain again

## *What I Give Back*

# In Concert

Carved from the goodness of women
I dance on a stage --Sure that
Dancing alone
I am the event -- the fruition
Of Goodness and Grace
Of Music and Movement
Of Poetry and Prose --
Then I bow to the women
In the front row

    Who screamed as I leapt
    From their womb but
    Now watch with eyes immortal --
    As I find myself in their gaze
    I see their reflection
    Their faces in my poetry --
    And I dance until the
    Whir of my pirouette
    Shakes the stars from the sky --
    While I ever spinning
    Weave a ribbon of rhyme
    Through the hands of the
    Women In the front row

        Then I gather the ribbon
        Back into my soul
        Fusing the stardust
        The women
        And me
        In the gossamer shelter
        Of each other's arms
        To dance together again
        Through Row
        After row
        After row

## *I'll Always Be With Them*

---

# Her Life's Sentence

Had she stayed at Holyoke
She may have broken the solitude
Escaped into a relationship
And become accustomed
To society's parlors
Not just her own

But for the sake of poetry
She shut her door to society
That bound scripture to religion
And put in its place
The splendor of a crown

Crowned by her own accord
She yielded her spirit to verse
And wed in a smock of white
Made each day a ceremony to an
Immaculate Conception of Words

The fruit of her union
Set nature to music
In a score whose rhythms
Beat as gently as a tipsy bee or
An invading morning dew

By leaving the world she found it
Spying from the inside out
She penned its composition
Into *Bolts of Melody*
With words like diadems
That time made her very own

## *I FOUND A BETTER WORLD WHEN I LEFT THIS BEHIND*

# Casual Magic

Like it just happens... Yeah
Casual magic happens whenever
It blows the top off of regular magic
A magician in a suit...how astute
A rabbit in a hat, what's that
A lady cut in half... Pahlease

Casual magic isn't tied to a stage
Rather it's a random prize
Taking you by surprise
Widening your eyes
No calculation just improvisation

It gives the whole idea of magic
A kick in the abstract because
It doesn't know where it's going
Poetry happens like casual magic
Writing itself down, coming back around
Until it's a rhyme but it doesn't happen
In regular time, rhyme happens in a
Casual sort of rhyme time

When Poetry happens
It calls for the Knighting of words
And the sprinkling of them upon
The royal page like laurels

Poetry is the act of rejoicing in
The casual magic of life -- it is
What we celebrate when we pull
Poesy from behind the looking glass
Or behind the ear of a grasshopper
Or when we cut a dangling participle
In half or make prose disappear
Into poetry... like this

## SOMETIMES I'M BETTER OFF NOT KNOWING WHERE CERTAIN THINGS ARE GOING, LIKE...

# Stepping Out

A Poet has a Master Key
It unlocks a Secret Door
The Bard is all Anticipation
Lest there be no more

Lest no more Feeling
And no more Rhyme
Stand behind the
Door of Time

Lest no more Playful
Syncopation
Thrive inside the Mind's
Elation

That once brought Homer's
God's of age
And Shakespeare's plays
Onto the Stage

Lo, let there always be a Key
A Struggling Poet just like me
A Door that opens onto Time
A Song of Universal Rhyme

# *I HOPE TO KEEP THAT PART OF ME THAT ALLOWS ME TO...*

_____

_____

_____

_____

_____

_____

_____

_____

_____

_____

_____

_____

_____

_____

_____

_____

_____

_____

_____

_____

_____

_____

_____

# The Literary Lift

There's a place where I go in my reverie
In the soft, smooth shade of my past
I cast my mind into its soothing vision
When my thoughts can take a holiday

I slip down to the riverfront
And walk with history along its banks
Giving thanks for her legacy
Of tradition and education

I amble up the levee to city streets
Toward the campus grounds
Where sounds of students echo
The age old song of youth's expectation

Great Halls loom behind gnarling trees
Whose wrought iron fences can't enclose
What grows and grows and grows
In my relaxed imagination

The majestic Spirit of St. Louis Past
Exhilarating in its literary lift
A gift that offers my vacationing thoughts
A forever hope and fascination

# MY SPECIAL PLACE TO FIND A LIFT IS

_____

_____

_____

_____

_____

_____

_____

_____

_____

_____

_____

_____

_____

_____

_____

_____

_____

_____

_____

_____

_____

_____

_____

*...And for a robe,*
*About her lank and all o'erteemed loins,*
*A blanket in the alarm of fear caught up --*

## Of Hide and Hamlet

*Who's there?*
Under layers of experience
Ever unfolding, changing
The color of your coat

As though it were
*Too much in the sun*
Dragginh your coat
Across a lifetime

Forever seeking ways to
Bury it so that
No one ever sees
Its true colors

Wonder
The outcome
For a needy world
If we simply wore our coats

Like the trees
Wear their rings
Marking each distinctive
Year of growth

Like the fall leaves
Wear their color
Whether burnt umber
Or golden
Like discoveries
Lay bear a history
Of research
Failed and famous

Like tiers of rock
Make mountains
From which we fall
To which we ascend

Like all the collective
Wisdom of the ages
Flaunts mistakes that
Preclude new accuracies

Were we to prance
Around as boldly
Wearing our coats of
Custom made experiences
We too would unfurl
Rings of life achievements
Colors proud and modest
Constant newness of spirit
Knowledge right and wrong
Grit like layers of granite

Were we to wear our coats
We would unleash
A humanity free to answer
The bard's timeless question
*To be, or not to be --*
And we would answer
"I'd be proud to engage
you later in this flap,
but for now may I
please just have my wrap?"

# MY COAT IS MADE OF...
## OR
## DOES ANYBODY CARE ABOUT SHAKESPEARE ANYMORE

_____

_____

_____

_____

_____

_____

_____

_____

_____

_____

_____

_____

_____

_____

_____

_____

_____

_____

_____

_____

_____

_____

_____

_____

_____

_____

_____

_____

# I Shall Not Be Contained

Eternal Rhythms
You invade - inhabit my very self
Arranging words side by side
On the scaffold of a stanza

But I must find my own way
Outside of your rules
Lay my words upon the stars
To shine beyond the page

I'd rather be lost in the
Recesses of space than think
That mindless correctness
I would ever embrace

My poetry escapes this world
for a quarry in the sky
And I, I chase it
Like a treasure seeker

I follow it to a place outside
Dimension and Eternity
And after a long day of creation
I find my way home again

# *I'm Different I'm Different – I Don't Always Conform*

_____

_____

_____

_____

_____

_____

_____

_____

_____

_____

_____

_____

_____

_____

_____

_____

_____

_____

_____

_____

_____

_____

_____

# Picture Perfect

By example
The Earth teaches us to be careful
After all
It has never spun off its axis
Or blown up
Or been arrested for conduct
Unbecoming a planet
Quite the contrary
It has maintained a reputable spin for eons

This old steadfast Earth teaches us that
No matter what happens,
Immediate threat from meteorites
Supernova explosions
UFO's on the event horizon
No matter what happens,
We must stay on axis
For, if we fall, we'll definitely
Lose our stride

Loosing stride is actually
Worse than loosing face
Because it takes a chunk out
A chunk that belonged there
When a chunk is missing
The void plays havoc
With bodily affairs so that
The picture of Man, the picture
Of Earth is missing a piece.

The picture is in the cave of
Humanity's very beginning
It shows all of us with
The moon and stars
And all the ideas we've
Collected for centuries
It's Plato's cave actually
And many think
The photo's really there

In this universal snapshot
We don't stand in groups
We don't stand in tribes
Or ethnic groups
Or nuclear families
Or cultural groups
Or races or skin colors
Tallest in the back or gender
We just stand together

Everyone looks just great
Except for Adam and Eve
And a few others villains
That history has ID'd
As having some kind
Of smudge on their face
Some original sin that
Cannot be forgiven
Unbelievable!

So whenever there is a smudge
They say it creates a missing
Chunk in the picture
And it throws off the whole thing
But then again, there
Could always be another twist
Maybe the philosophy is flawed,
Maybe I'm all wrong
And there is no cave

It could simply be a blurry lens
Or just a mechanical glitch
That fractures the chunk theory
But listen, I'm going to get
Some wallet size family pictures
So you can carry the whole
Clan around with you
Looking at it occasionally may
Keep you out of the dark room

# *My Picture of Life Is...*

_____

_____

_____

_____

_____

_____

_____

_____

_____

_____

_____

_____

_____

_____

_____

_____

_____

_____

_____

_____

_____

_____

# Reach Into The Light

My poems are Spirals
Spun by an Apprentice Spider
Innocently Seeking
The Soul inside her
Where Angels rule with propriety
But shut the door on that Society

Free of decorum I knock
At the Door of Mystery
*Emily's Circumference*
Where I'm free to frolic
To be transported to the
Eye of the Poem to discover
What she found at the Center

Where Philosophy and Truth
Commingle in Verse
Where Molecules of Sacred
Meaning long ensnared
In Silken Superstrings
Strike like lightning across
A canvass of air

And in this clapping light
Muses reveal their stash of silk
Unraveling under steady watch
A glimpse of the sublime
And I Poet Postulant
Have one chance to weave it
Into the Canon of Rhyme

# *I Reach For Meaning When I...*

# The Day I Heard The Platform Of
# The Mayor of Boylston Massachusetts

The generous pines greeted me.
  The copper-colored tree tops
tossed chilly, wet leaves at my feet,
  and a far-off Robin chirped
the day's docket to a rising sun:

*"Shine down on pine needles*
  *that fall to the ground.*
*Warm them without any sound,*
  *for in silence they knit*
*with pointed precision*
  *a golden blanket all around."*

"And heat up the tree tops,"
  cried the boisterous song bird.
*"They too have a job,"* he said.
*"They color my floor*
*where I perch in the night*
  *on a carpet of autumn red.*

*In tree tops I hide my breast*
  *from all other birds at large,*
*who do not know the sun like me*
  *and do not understand my charge.*

*It's not easy to rule the sunshine*
  *because sometimes no matter what*
*it just pops up and makes its sweep*
  *when I know the pines*
*want a little more sleep*
  *and the tree tops aren't ready*
*to unfurl the red rug*
  *that keeps me warm, and safe, and snug.*

*Nevertheless, I am the boss.  Most*
  *evenings it doesn't make a peep.*
*That big, warm bear up in the sky*
  *simply sets when I sing it to sleep."*

*"The politics of the morning,"* he said,
  *"and the politics of the night,*
*are sometimes too much for a Robin*
  *whose elected to govern the light.*

*"Tho I've been told by supporters*
*  that its good when we make choices*
*when a bird like me goes out on a limb*
*  to represent silent voices.*

*But if I get too selfish*
*  it's the job of the rest of creation*
*to vote me out of my perch*
*  or risk degradation.*

*And I would go quite gladly.*
*  I'm a red-breasted Robin with pride*
*I must govern a kingdom that wants me*
*  it's there I should preside.*

*However, my good friends of Boylston*
*  I'm early, I've brought you the worm*
*and tonight,  I say,  because of this*
*  I shall seek another term."*

### *And If I Get Too Selfish*

_____

_____

_____

_____

_____

_____

_____

_____

_____

_____

_____

_____

_____

_____

# Notes

# Offering II

## Acknowledging new dimensions of myself

## Talked About
## By Lovers To This Day

There's a Poetry

In Romance

Two beats of

Different Measure

Come together

In a magical way

Like binary stars revolve

Around each other

In a Dance of Desire

Until two separate

Rhythms blend

In one Hopeless Devotion

In one Pulsing Light

In one Fascinating Rhythm

In One Poem

Written by Destiny

Spoken by Silent Eyes

Published by the Wind

Read by Moonlight

Marveled at by the

Whole Milky Way

## MY DANCE OF DESIRE

---

---

---

---

---

---

---

---

---

---

---

---

---

---

---

---

---

---

---

---

---

---

---

---

---

---

---

---

---

# Roses Are Red

A Rose by any other name
Is still a rose, they say

But me, I change like clouds
Then I'm no longer me

I turn into a raging bull
Then lose my horns quite fast

For a moment I am me
But I was her in the dreadful past

Tomorrow I'll be someone else
Maybe just a she

Looking in a mirror cracked
For what is left of me

Rose, your name is Scarlet,
Tender, Budding, Red

Your name is Second Hand, my dear
When you're trampled or half dead

So the point is, Rose
You're just like me

You're many
Though you're one

A Rose by any other name...
My blushing blossom, is just a pun

## *I Have Many Names*

# Seams Familiar

There is a voice inside my head

I do not know its source

I only know the words it speaks

Are for eternity


In a whirling spiral they take wing

Untwisting the future

Making sense out of the abyss

Like chaos shapes a sound


Poetry is from the Gods

I know not their address

It may be postmarked Time or Space

Or simply Nothingness

## THE VOICE INSIDE
## MY HEAD SAYS...

# The Urge To Write

Once begun there is no let up
Coming in waves
It's relentless
Staying longer and longer
Until it becomes its host

Acting the menace
Yet deferring to mood
It gorges
On sights and sounds
It wails in moonlight

Feeding off the poet's
Blood -- It knows pain
And eventually
Consumes her crystal breath

*"I'm not heartless.  I cry for her as*
*I lurk in the shadows.*
*I know I can stop her any time*
*But I would rather see her*
*Worked to the bone.*
*That's when she is satisfied.*
*I love to watch her as she*
*Sews rhymes among the clouds*
*Dropping seeds on wings of birds*
*Who carry her kernels*
*Of poetry to places unknown.*
*I know that as long as I'm alive*
*She'll walk inside history*
*Tended to and cared for --*
*Never alone."*

# WHAT CONSUMES
## MY BREATH?

_____

_____

_____

_____

_____

_____

_____

_____

_____

_____

_____

_____

_____

_____

_____

_____

_____

_____

_____

_____

_____

_____

_____

_____

_____

_____

_____

# The Tao of the Mud Dauber

Miss Mud Dauber
Has a Slant on Life
Physically and Psychologically

    She has a bent for mud
    Or crud, or any appearance of mud

*"Lye Low*
*Lye Low,"*
 she whispers

Simply put, she indulges in dirt
Stays close to the Earth
Her constitution is clay

    She has an inclination toward soil
    To toil and boil her eggs in soil

*"Lye Low*
*Lye Low,"*
 she whispers


But why does the Wasp Woman
Seek such depths
Instead of dallying on high

    She must have a bond with the ground
    Or be bound by vows with the ground

*"Lye Low*
*Lye Low,"*
 she whispers

What say you Miss to this
*"In mud I won't fall,"* she says. *"For me it's win-win.*
*My little progeny are without original sin."*

Although she's just a puddle-hopping vamp
There's no sign of stain in her camp

*"Lye Low*
*Lye Low..."*
she whispers

## MY WIN-WIN

_____

_____

_____

_____

_____

_____

_____

_____

_____

_____

_____

_____

_____

_____

_____

_____

_____

_____

_____

_____

_____

# Between Here and Thereafter

On the way to Boston

A deserved vacation

I see trees stand like sentries

To proclaim probation

From all the routines

Of everyday life

Retreat from the dreaded

Carbuncle "Strife"

We're off to walk

The Freedom Trail

Just like the guys

Who saved our tail

Then forward again

Destinations unknown

Forward toward death

Each Patriot -- Alone

# *THOUGH I WALK THROUGH THE VALLEY...*

# Tick Tock Game's Locked

Try to stop a clock from ticking

Or halt a raging storm

Grab a spot off of a leopard

See what happens to your arm


It's folly to chase your shadow

Or paddle up the stream

Creation's cards have all been dealt

It's better just to dream

# *MY FOLLY*

_____

_____

_____

_____

_____

_____

_____

_____

_____

_____

_____

_____

_____

_____

_____

_____

_____

_____

_____

_____

_____

_____

_____

_____

## Words Happen

My life has not been very exciting
It doesn't top any social charts
Yet the life in my mind
Expands and contracts
More rhythmically than my pulse  ~~
I ask myself at times
Am I more poetry than flesh and blood
Why can't I write courtroom dramas
Or emergency room theatrics
Or even news articles ~~
When I try
I keep coming back to an old haunt
A place that's familiar to me
Mysterious to me
It's the center of words themselves ~~
If I can't climb inside the words
I'm not satisfied
The happenings outside the words
Never fit me
They fall short of – Wonderment ~~
Poetry makes me wonder what's next
Real things that happen seem
Well, over as soon as they begin
But words hold divine intrigue
I want to search their innards ~~
Were I a word psychiatrist
I would Quake at their thoughts
Were I a word doctor
I would Gasp at their composition
Or a word surgeon, I'd be Cut into pieces ~~
And if I were ever to be a poet
I would just Die of excitement
It's best that I just write

## *I Return To My Old Haunt*

# Being Young

Youth has no finish line
Only the track ahead
That holds the promise of
Excitement and achievement
Encounters with other horses
Either swift or long running

Youth is wrapped in promise
In a bridle of anticipation
Of a fresh start
It dashes from the gait
Eager to run with the herd who
Enter impetuous into the race

Youth puts the trot to the test
Until all fours are off the ground
In suspended animation
Elastic in a rigid world
Ecstatic from an ego that thinks
Eventually will never come

# *I Know This Feeling*

# Poetry Is

Poetry is the universe tending her sheep

Poetry is history's refrain

Poetry is evolution snickering over slow progress

Poetry is law smirking when it works

Poetry is motion giggling at its own rhythm

Poetry is happiness revealing itself in the mirror

Poetry is medicine beaming over its cures

Poetry is inhibition fading into personality

Poetry is the millennium getting a chance to happen

Poetry is a lover waiting to be smitten

Poetry is the environment breathing easy

Poetry is putting a clean coat of paint on the alphabet

Poetry is nature talking back

Poetry is the peaceful coexistence of opposing words

Poetry is politics caring for all of the above

# FOR ME POETRY IS...

_____

_____

_____

_____

_____

_____

_____

_____

_____

_____

_____

_____

_____

_____

_____

_____

_____

_____

_____

_____

_____

_____

_____

_____

_____

_____

_____

# The Anchor Woman

Camera ready
She's at the station
Her head is spinning
With information

She must do her best
And she can't be late
She's in a man's world
Her job is at stake

She spins in her chair
She grabs the mike
Holy cow her lipstick
Looks a fright

It's too late the red
Light is flashing its sign
*Ten seconds to go*
*Is everything fine?*

"God no," she yells,
"my make-up is wrong.
Throw in a filler;
play a song."

The crew starts to scramble
She slips from her chair
The powder goes flying
All over her hair

She bites her tongue
The song's almost through
There's blood on her nose
What the hell should she do

She pulls herself up
And collects her poise
looks straight in the camera
And makes a loud noise

"Good evening my friends
I've got great news.
Women no longer
have to pay dues.

I'm Humpty Dumpty
of Channel Five.
I've had a great fall
but I'm still alive.

You're looking at me

with my hair a mess,

and I don't care

If I tore my dress.


I don't care

If I'm worn and old.

I'll be myself,

I've broken the mold.


Tune in America.

Turn on your set.

Cause what you see

is what you get."

## A POEM FOR ME
## JUST FOR ME

_____

_____

_____

_____

_____

_____

_____

_____

_____

_____

_____

_____

_____

_____

_____

_____

_____

_____

_____

_____

_____

_____

_____

_____

# A Red Hot City Block

City streets flow in my veins

Bricks and mortar consume

The better part of my soul


I love the sight of row houses

Gleaming Red in the evening sun

Emitting the day's heat


The grey cracked sidewalks

Home to incorrigible weeds

And clumps of green Easter moss


But now the city lacks its alluring Red

It's all steel and no heart  -  gone the

Sandy tracks of shuffle boards


Smells of ash pits -  sawdust

Buckets of foamy beer

And back alley hollyhocks

# *WHERE I LIVED*

---
---
---
---
---
---
---
---
---
---
---
---
---
---
---
---
---
---
---
---
---
---
---
---
---
---
---
---
---
---
---

# China Doll

Lost inside porcelain

In pinafore and lace

I sat disconnected

Alone, out of place

*I dangled my legs*

*From the shelf...*

The cold enamel paint

Of the wooden ledge

Held me fast in a

Shadow box world

Where I stared

Through antiseptic eyes

At gnarled attitudes

And ritual despair

*I dangled my legs*

*From the shelf...*

They were the only

Part of me that moved

Going to sleep on occasion

As they dangled there

But I never let a tear

Interrupt the white cheek

The constant play of terror

Or the cast iron ritual


*I dangled my legs*
*From the shelf...*


I sat undisturbed

Till the sun faded my lace

Jostling knocked me over

And the porcelain bled

I bled for years

Cold white streams

Dry heaving cells

Till nothing was left, yet

*I dangled my legs*

*From the shelf...*


Till a slight motion

An ever so slight motion

Started a pale rose glow

In my creviced cheeks

And today my blood is Red

My thoughts leap

Outside my head

I'm glad I didn't stop

*I dangled my legs*

*From the shelf...*

# *STRESSED, ME? – I DON'T KNOW?*

_____
_____
_____
_____
_____
_____
_____
_____
_____
_____
_____
_____
_____
_____
_____
_____
_____
_____
_____
_____
_____
_____
_____
_____
_____
_____
_____
_____
_____
_____
_____

# Crete Paper Clips

I noticed two teenagers
Their cigarette smoke
Rising up into sunrays
Reminding me of the joyous
Feeling of being young
Of being so agreeable to life
That the whole world fits
Inside of a smile
With air that is always fresh
Blowing summer breezes
Consecrating all of life with fun...
With books on a sultry afternoon
A little light jazz playing
As the neighbor washes the car
Lemonade and the sweet smell
Of pear blossoms in the shade
A walk to school on Saturday
To hang out at the school yard
A whiff of bleached sheets
Flapping on a clothesline
Bike riding to nice neighborhoods
Where there are brick houses
A hike down railroad tracks

Until an apparition appears
Rising from hot tar
A game of pick-up baseball
So intense a dirt necklace forms
And sitting out on the porch with
A favorite comic book
A Coke at the corner confectionery
The distant drone of a lawnmower
A rainbow in the sprinkler
Then later a calm sleep so deep
That tomorrow's a light year away
As daydreams rise like smoke

In the light of a projector
Re-running sentimental thoughts
That lay around like toys in
The attic of my mind and
I go there often to resume

Those endless PG-rated days


## *Toys In My Attic*


_____

_____

_____

_____

_____

_____

_____

_____

_____

_____

_____

_____

_____

_____

_____

_____

_____

_____

_____

_____

# Notes

# Offering III

## Helping them make a better me

# Offsetting Motion

The gamut has a self-sustaining balance
For every bad there is an equalizing good
Though love abounds, evil lurks unhampered
Whether or not it should


One does not annihilate the other
Law can't keep disorder under tow
Chance perhaps weights opposing forces
To see how far off kilter each will go


The pendulum travels on a timeline
Nature holds it crucially on track
Could each future moment be offset
By the ability to go back

# *WOULD I GO BACK*
## *IF I COULD?*

_____

_____

_____

_____

_____

_____

_____

_____

_____

_____

_____

_____

_____

_____

_____

_____

_____

_____

_____

_____

_____

_____

_____

# Prospecting Poesy

The pursuit of my own mystery
Propels my soul
With a bold and giddy intrigue
Like a panner for hidden gold

I sift my blurry vision
Till I clear away the sty
Behold, I see the dusting
that hints deeper I must pry

Allured by apparition
I lurch deeper in my frame,
Back and forth from nothing
Whence the teasing glimmer came

I toil to exhaustion
Till all light is gone from me
And the only hoped- for treasure
Is Luminosity

But light comes in its own time
After poise has calmed my passion
Then rational the words appear
In literary fashion

To see like lightning golden
What holds my own story
Fragments of reality
Bits of gleaming glory

With awe and admiration
I receive them with a prayer
And polish them till flawlessly
They debut to the fair

# *MY OWN STORY*

# The Researcher's Mate

God didn't make any secrets

They occurred in their own course

And man in constant motion

Seeks their source


Bound by human instinct

And a bent toward mastery

Mankind journeys outward

And mates with mystery


Surrounded by newness

Nothing is sure

Yet in one magic moment

Stumbles on a cure


Then comes the real test

To see if they'll cope

With only each other

And a Promise of Hope

## *I Seek Newness*

# Seasoned

The unsuspecting soul
Ravaged by despair
And feeble intuition
Leaves imagination bare

Naive to spirits
That totally consume
His soul is quickly lost
To an alcoholic doom

He stands upon the shore
With a self that is eroding
Esteem that's losing ground
An inner voice exploding

Urged to throw into the sea
The one thing that he craves
He feels a sinking oneness
With the broken waves

Out of practice as Himself
Alone to face his will
He sees reflecting back at him
The part it couldn't kill

The part that was the thinker
But God it's hard to think
With this constant, cornered urge
To have a drink

After years of tuning out
And avoiding all the pain
It's his final chance
Not to die in vain

Maybe freedom only comes
After the soul's paid its dues
And the Exorcist Sea
Gives life after booze

## *I AM A CONQUEROR*

# Searching

I went out the back gate to go to school
Only three houses from the corner
Made a short walk to the alley
By the gate on the side fence were
Morning Glory's with such personality
I watched for them each morning and
As Maria said of Edelwiess
"Every morning you greet me...."

They were so beautiful
They were a true sky blue
With soft petals and milky centers
Splashing out from unruly green vines...
They were better than fireworks
I wanted them to stay open all day
At least till the Angelus
But they always went away...

Disintegrating like a camera flash
Leaving only a shadow of light
But the fleeting splashes of color
Found a home in me...
Color thou art
And to color thou shalt return
All the colors I've ever seen live in me now
Like the shadow of reality...

Blue has always given my life meaning
From the Sky to the Water
From Morning Glories to Fireworks
From Stained Glass to the Nun's Habits
From my eyes to the memories behind them
Of Splashing Blue Mornings
I carry the blue with me
And I still walk out back...

I still want them to rouse me
To pierce my consciousness
To make my silver reality new
And so as morning dawns
I recollect Morning Glory Blue
I live in both colorful worlds
Trying to find, trying to see
Trying to write, what's true...

## *THE COLOR OF MY LIFE IS...*

_____
_____
_____
_____
_____
_____
_____
_____
_____
_____
_____
_____
_____
_____
_____
_____
_____
_____
_____
_____

# The Silence of Innocence

The snow is just beginning to fall
Tiny and fast like a baby's breath
And before you know it
It has grown by inches

Forming like an infant into a child
The wind picks up and it blows
Into clumps of personality
Each snow fall is a Child of Nature

I celebrate its youth and beauty
It's white Untouched Innocence
I'm distracted by its joyful fantasy
Before it all begins to fade

Then as time sculptures beauty
Carving youth into grey lines
I lose the thrill of newness
And neglect the Youngster Slush

Until the streets are filled with the
Soot of Neglected Humanity
The once beautiful snow
Files into narrow gutters

Running into sewer death camps
Destroyed in the underground
While I, America, watch
The Holocoust of Snow

# *I Should Speak Up*

# Still to Come

I'm filled with thoughts
That can't get out
Filled with the mystery
Of what they're about

They're in my unconscious
Where they like to roam
But inside my rhyme
Is their real home

Wanting them with me
Hasn't always been my way
Perhaps my past denial
Is why they stay away

It was hard to be myself
To say what I really thought
Fear held me like the devil
I was always distraught

But now I want those thoughts
Yet I know their frustration
When they wanted me
My fear caused hesitation

I regret I didn't acknowledge them
So when they no longer roam
I'll spin them into poetry
And make them right at home

# *There's Room Left Inside My Heart*

# *An Emily Dickinson Riddle*

I wish I were Ghandi
I wish I could just stop
For a minute to really
Think straight
To think things through

What a luxury to have
The gift of leisure
But it wasn't leisure
That gave Gandhi insight
It was control
So I will work to have
Command of myself
Because I know that
I do not have it now
Self Control is what
The nuns used to say
Have self control

Don't give in to
Your wants and desires
I guess I'll start by not
Wanting to be like Gandhi
But the paradox is
That only leaves wanting
To be...

Who am I?

## *Who Do I Want To Be?*

_____

_____

_____

_____

_____

_____

_____

_____

_____

_____

_____

_____

_____

_____

_____

_____

_____

_____

_____

_____

_____

_____

_____

_____

_____

# Clarity

Now that I'm older
I've lost gray matter
Literally
I see in black and white
This is a result of the onset
Of floaters
Tiny specks of black
On any white background
The specks are annoying
They force me to discriminate
In order to differentiate
But they have an upside
I must focus more deeply now
Upon a million things
That come into my view
I have you might say
A new perspective
Especially regarding racism
How literal it is to see
Anything in only Black and White
How annoying

# *I FOCUS MORE NOW ON...*

# Comings and Goings

Corporations are vanishing
Corruption is flourishing

Crows are vanishing
Chemicals are flourishing

Competency is vanishing
Campaigns are flourishing

Cathedrals are vanishing
Campuses are flourishing

Cabooses are vanishing
Cars are flourishing

Convents are vanishing
Casinos are flourishing

Cellulose is vanishing
Cosmetics are flourishing

Cities are vanishing
Capitalism is flourishing

Civil Liberties are vanishing
Censorship is flourishing

Circumcisions are vanishing
C-Sections are flourishing

Comedy is vanishing
Cynicism is flourishing

Change remains Constant

## *I CAN'T STOP TO WAIT*
## *FOR CHANGE*

_____

_____

_____

_____

_____

_____

_____

_____

_____

_____

_____

_____

_____

_____

_____

_____

_____

_____

_____

_____

_____

_____

_____

_____

# In Defense of Clichés

I find the happiest people
Can be those with the least

~~~~~

Least is sometimes good
It cancels out greed
In a way that defines it
If I analyze least
I find hunger
For relevant basics
And that "Nothing from
Nothing is Nothing"

~~~~~

If I analyze greed
I find hunger
For Irrelevant riches
And that hunger for
Riches is nothing*ness*
So the new expression
"Greed is good" - is true
It's good for nothing

# THE GRASS ALWAYS SEEMS GREENER...

_____

_____

_____

_____

_____

_____

_____

_____

_____

_____

_____

_____

_____

_____

_____

_____

_____

_____

_____

_____

_____

_____

_____

_____

_____

_____

_____

# Nova Pro Nobis

Poetry is the star
To which I hitch my wagon
My wagon is filled
With second rate verses
That no one will ever read
But the star is so bright
I can't stop gazing at it
I can't stop the journey
Toward the source of its sound

    The infinite resounding
    Silence in my head
    Explodes into the mystery
    Of where the poem starts
    And where it goes and
    When it's finally heard
    What happens then
    What is affected by it
    Who is forever changed

Perhaps I have hitched my wagon
To the ultimate universal question
What is Poetry
And I happen to know
The answer to this one
Very important question
"What is it made of?"
Wait for it...
Poetry is made of stardust

    It led the Magi
    It wrote the Magnificat
    It lives in Me

# I HITCH MY WAGON TO...

_____

_____

_____

_____

_____

_____

_____

_____

_____

_____

_____

_____

_____

_____

_____

_____

_____

_____

_____

_____

_____

_____

_____

_____

_____

_____

_____

_____

# Skeptic or Sinner

I often wonder
What will happen to me
When I die
For I've all but lost
My faith in the next world
I can't find any evidence
Of the next world
Only this one
How fickle I am having
Grown up "religious"
Believing in the
Afterlife for so many
Years and now I
Search for that once
And glorious faith
I have become a
Doubting Thomas
I wonder too about
Thomas' integrity
Faith they say can
Move a mountain so
Why can't it move doubt

# *I Doubt That...*

# Poetry's Prophesy

The 21<sup>st</sup> Century

Can it really be upon us

I mistakenly thought

It would bring a

New Spirit of Civilization

Mournfully it has not

Instead we make war

Around the globe

As though we've lost our

Collective enlightenment

Oh Muse of Poetry

Have mercy on us

Say not that you have

Ended your eternal vigil

You who consecrate the

Rhythms of the universe

Inspire us anew to restore

The words that prophesize

Your legitimate progeny

~~ Peace ~~

# *I Am A Creator Of Peace*

We've written together about the birds, those glorious, high-minded creatures that we so often take for granted. It's time to treasure them not look down upon their small size or fragile delicacy. After all we humans haven't mastered their art in the sky. It's time we took them seriously. It's time to open our hearts to the enlightenment they want to share with us.

## A Dove Called Francis

The birds amassed by the droves
Thousands maybe millions of birds
Landing on every telephone line in sight
While bandit sun rays shifted in the breeze
And the sky took a selfie
Of its own perfect blue

    This plenary gathering of birds
    Waited patiently to begin
    Of course patience is in their DNA
    Finding worms is a game of patience
    So they bobbed and watched and waited
    When suddenly the sky opened up

And descending down toward them
Through lustrous pearly clouds came
A dove – with feathers of white
And a kindly sparkle in his eyes
He landed in the midst of the birds
Greeting them in the comforting
Cooing words that only he could express

He conversed with them for some time
And he stayed with them a while
Flitting up and down the wires
Visiting every species of bird
Spending time with baby birds
And birds that were sick

His gentle caring so affected the birds
They cuddled closer on the lines
Looked at each other with loving eyes
And burst into song
A psalm heard around the world

~~~~~~~~

*You came into our hearts*
*Now as we return to our nests*
*Our spirits are refreshed*
*You helped us understand we're*
*More than feather and bone*
*And so that none will be alone*
*Our wings we shall interweave*
*We'll fly together and perceive*
*The presence of God in our sky*
*It is our spirit that makes us fly*
                *Thus we say*
*With confidence in our breast*
*Ubi Caritas est vera, Deus ibi est*

~~~~~~~~~

And after the song they joined wings
Taking care to intertwine their feathers
Carefully so none would break
And they lifted off in sets of hundreds
Filling the sky like lined paper
And the baby birds flew in
The shelter of their mother's wings
And the sick little birds were woven
Tightly into the hearts of these
Black squadrons on a mission to
Make them well as only caring
And kindred birds could do

And as they began to fade away
Dropping into the Eastern sky
They bowed to the horizon
Before saying good-bye

~~~~~~~~~

# *I OPEN MY HEART TO THE WORLD*

# The Time Weaver

As a teacher of literature I deal with
The concept of time in narration
A master writer, I allege,
Weaves from past to present
A master writer can manipulate time so
Cleverly that a story can move from
Fiction to Science Fiction
It's been a mechanistic lecture until
I saw time weaving with my own eyes
I saw nature show herself to be
Not just master but Monarch of Time
This autumn we had an unusually hot spell
Two of my Sugar Maples began to turn
In Late September
Long before the October blaze
But the Red Maple did a funny thing
It lost all of its leaves
Then tiny buds began to form and
It sprouted new leaves
How independent of that little tree
How untimely to enter into Spring
When it was clearly Fall
If this were prose I could explain
The author's manipulation, purpose
And motivation to interfere in the
Time cycle of the seasons
But there is no author of this story
Except for One

# *I MUST TAKE TIME TO...*

# Notes

# Offering IV

## The shape my spirit is in

# The Writer's Life

My life is about small things
Germs of ideas that lead to
Tiny particles of ink on a page
That turn into seeds of thought

Twelve point fonts that transform
Ink into minute sparks of electricity
Forming a stanza on the screen for
Those germinal seeds of thought

Little postage stamps affixed
To standard size envelopes
That are my transport for
Those germinal seeds of thought

Slight happy moments opening
Letters that say congratulations
We'll take a chance and buy your seeds
We think they'll make a fine garden

# *I Want To Celebrate Everything I Can*

# Lost and Found

So Eve
Why did you let it get so far?
What were you thinking?

Even if some guy reporter
Was listening at the garden gate
You should have done something.

All of us
All of recorded history
Holds you responsible

For letting a story
About a stupid rib
Make it down through the ages

Without so much as a protest
Without even a peep
For posterity

Well, you might want to know
That despite the story by the first reporter
We've done pretty well

So well, that young women don't think
About glass ceilings, subservience,
Inequality and especially not rib stories

About the real garden story, Eve
You should have told us what the reporter
Was doing snooping around anyway

Paparazzi, press corps, media nose wagons
Eden eavesdroppers, they can mess up history
When they don't get it straight

Lucky we found your journal recently
So we can clear this matter up
It will be broadcast news this evening

*"Eve's Private Diary Found.*
*Story of Creation Comes Under Scrutiny.*
*Eve Claims She Had Things Under Control*
*When Adam Was Knee High To A Snake."*    *UPI*

### *TRUTH IS STRANGER THAN...*

_____
_____
_____
_____
_____
_____
_____
_____
_____
_____
_____
_____
_____
_____
_____
_____
_____
_____
_____
_____
_____
_____

# Take 1

A room
With a bed
And a brass railing
A window, closed
A man staring
Looking at nothing
In particular but
Time
Facing off with
The glare of the sun
That attacks him
Through slanted blinds
On the closed window
He wears a tan suit
And next to him
Rising gray and directionless
Cigarette smoke
The hallmark of the 40's
    Man -- two inch blinds
     -- suit -- room --
    And smoke that is
    Free to plot it's own course
    Free to filter through
    Time and bent sunrays
    Freedom in the 40's when
    There was still time to think
    Of the desperate future when
    There was still time to watch
    Ourselves
    Living out our own dramas
    When
    Most importantly to
    The eternal scene of life
    There was
    In The 40's
    Still time

# *TAKE 1, THAT'S ALL LIFE GIVES,*
## *JUST ONE  TRY AT IT*

# Rounding Off

The circularity of motion
Makes the bell toll –

The bell signals and
Man responds with Ceremony

Ceremony honors the Creator
Who authored the Circle of Life

From steel to plaster
From sound to flesh

From ritual to ideal
From Center to Edge

Life circles and
Life cycles and

The Circularity of Motion
Shapes the Soul

## *My Life Is A Circle Of...*

_____

_____

_____

_____

_____

_____

_____

_____

_____

_____

_____

_____

_____

_____

_____

_____

_____

_____

_____

_____

_____

_____

_____

_____

# Turning Into Each Other

Fantastic are the long-winged birds
The waves that beat the shore
Invading with their wings and sound
The poet's "Evermore"

Rushing through the barriers
That space and time have made
To keep the sky above the sea
To keep the sea afraid

Afraid to swell and slap the shore
To embrace the winged knave
To spray him with a bubbly foam
And ride him on the wave

For when the bird and sea are one
It's then the sea can fly
The bird dips in the ocean blue
And finger-paints the sky

The landscape indiscernible
Is fluid, flying, wet
The sea, the sky, the gulls are lost
From the moment that they met

# I Am One With

# Hide and Seek

Dickinson made riddles
So shall I
What say you is the best sound


The tinkling of piano keys
The drip, drip, drip of rain
The coo of a newborn baby
A dog barking in the distance
Natalie Cole
Somewhere a train whistle
The wind rushing through clover
The rustle of your mother's dress
Voices in the kitchen
Snow-laden pines scratching the roof
A belly laugh
Typewriter keys clicking away
Frank Sinatra
The words "I love you"


Answer:
The one you still hear

# *WHEN I HEAR THE MUSIC OF...*

# Pregnant

*adj.* Bearing issue
Or results; fruitful; prolific


As I sit here reading poetry
Reading about poetry

I remember one of those
Crystal bits of information

That hit me like an iceberg
Cracks an unconscious brain

Simply told, as are all great ideas
It was that the writing of poetry

Is really one continuous
Movement of the pen

Each new poem simply jumps
Off from the word of the last

So as I write, I continually recreate
Different versions of the same poem

I wonder does a woman
Continually give birth

To different versions
Of the same child

Do we both pick up stitches
From the same thread

Spinning DNA and poesy
From the same ball of yarn

Plowing through life's
Rhymes and reasons

Until one day at
Completion, magically

The face of the ultimate design
Reveals itself at last

## I NEVER THOUGHT ABOUT...

_____
_____
_____
_____
_____
_____
_____
_____
_____
_____
_____
_____
_____
_____
_____
_____
_____
_____
_____
_____

# Teaching English

It's really not so much for them as me

It lets the muse escape in controlled measure

As opposed to writing poetry

When the muse flies at random


    One is the retail racket

    And the other the wholesale whimsy

    Of words


It's really not so much for them as me

The retail keeps me harnessed

The poetry makes me wild

The two worlds seldom converge


    For one is the business

    And the other the playground

    Of words

# WHAT MAKES ME WILD?

# A Secondary Occupation

It seemed every time she spoke
She became undone
Rehearsals weren't effective
    When the curtain rose
    Somewhere in her mind
    She tried to breathe
    But only inadequacy
    Stepped into the light

There were no confidant lines
And no means of being discreet
No peaceful poise
    What filled the room
    Was questioning looks
    Unfulfilled expectations
    Sighs of impatience
    From the other party

And the other party
Never having perfected
Consideration would say,
    "Can you speak up?"
    But she could not
    There had been too much
    Previously
    That had gone on

Too much on her nerves

She would see a counselor

Try to find composure

    Her personal arrangement

    Her composition, after all

    Was a relative thing

    Perhaps she'd find calm

    As a writer

## THE PRICE WE PAY

_____

_____

_____

_____

_____

_____

_____

_____

_____

_____

_____

_____

_____

_____

_____

_____

_____

_____

_____

# What Poetry Is

It is the soul unscrambling

One thread at a time –

Trying to reveal its very core

Which is so good, so immensely

Good, that the sheer force of it

Explodes in one creative act –

Spiraling, unraveling,

Exacting from itself

What it's made of –


Divinity splitting

Into a new universe

With each word

## *A New Word, A New Thought,*
## *A New Day, A New Me...*

# The Second Millennium Around

From the corset
To the computer
From the Model-T
To the missile
We have advanced
In material matters –
We do less physically
No strings to tie
On the corset
No motors to crank
On the Model-T –
Mostly we push
Buttons these days

We have discarded the
Strings and cranks
We have found
Fluoride and aspirin
And we're all quite happy
From our St. John's Wort –
But when will we advance
In matters of the heart
Why, I ask a shooting star
After a Millennium
Can't we get the simplest
Of messages straight –

--Love One Another—

# MY HEART'S SEDATIVE

_____

_____

_____

_____

_____

_____

_____

_____

_____

_____

_____

_____

_____

_____

_____

_____

_____

_____

_____

_____

_____

_____

_____

_____

_____

_____

_____

# The Shape Of Things To Come

The poem itself
Is a spiral of meaning
That by inference
Must come back to its beginning
To be reborn as something
That can be sensed –
Something – "sensible"
The sensibility
In its lucidity
Seeps into the poet
Gestates
And pushes out like
A bubble escapes the sea
Slow, exquisite,
Mighty in the light
Still Elongated,
Stunned by air
Struggling for shape
Seeking its own clarity
Searching for a place
To float independently
Until it enters
Someone else's intellect
Whole, victorious,
In perfect circle

# I'm Always Becoming

# Attic Chatter

They were permanently retired
Living in the Penthouse
Having the time of their lives
They talked from morning till night
About the Old Days mostly
About the way things used to be

They loved Communal Living
Said it was healthy
Staying with Your Own Kind

They enjoyed cleaning tarnished brass
As they listened to old War Songs
Or a good Sousa March
And when they danced
They loved the stiff, upright
Movements of the Waltz

The Silent Butler stood by the stairs
He loved standing watch
And serving all the others

On Holidays they would get visitors
Not always polite folks
Some asked embarrassing questions
Prying over personal things
Like a person's background
Or the way a body ages

Such rudeness
There's Propriety you know
Some things are best left to history

Young folks shouldn't come around
Acting like others are
Antiques or something
Shhh, someone's coming
Pull the shrouds over your heads

## *PASSING ON*
### *AND*
## *PASSING JUDGMENT*

---
---
---
---
---
---
---
---
---
---
---
---
---
---
---
---
---
---
---
---
---
---
---
---

# Because She Could Not Stop For Death She Jumped In Me

An old-fashioned girl
Sings of nature's gifts
Stating things simply
Sure of approval
She begins to speak
Goosebumps peak
And her sound
Is as smooth
As the fuzz
That hits your teeth
Before the peach does --
The pulpy words
Satiate
    They are tangy
        They satisfy
        They teach
        The thought of them
        Makes me hunger
        For a peach
        Wouldn't she laugh
        At this silly rhyme
        By an old-fashioned girl
        Who makes verse with haste
        As if it were in good taste
        She and I move swiftly through
        An orchard of poetry
        Waiting to be picked
        Because she wouldn't be tricked
        By Death

# *I Vow*
## *to Have More Fun*

# Notes

# Offering V

## Enjoying a new sense of myself

# Behind the Scenes

Standing on a Wooden Bridge
In Spanish Lake Park
Gazing out upon
The Lake's endless ripples
I saw a duck
Suspended
In trouble
Ducks don't just sit still
They duck around –
A Park Ranger rode up just then
On the most gorgeous black
Steed I'd ever seen
I said, "I think one of your
ducks is in trouble;
it's not moving."
The ranger quickly dismounted
And waded in toward the duck
I walked away, satisfied
Later I saw his silhouette
Reflected
On the other side of the lake
Galloping along
Silently
Down the pencil, tree-lined path --
Having seen the strength
Of his tenderness
I was struck with emotion
Awed by the beauty of ebony
Streaking through the trees
It was as though an artist
Had painted him into the picture
Of my life that day --
The Artist In the Lake
Lived beneath a wet canvass

His pictures splashed upon my brain
In flame and pastel
I won't forget the Ranger
The Ebony Day
And the liquid, rippling stallion
From the Underside of Art

## *WHEN I'M ALONE*

_____

_____

_____

_____

_____

_____

_____

_____

_____

_____

_____

_____

_____

_____

_____

_____

_____

_____

_____

_____

# Cicada Citadel

Standing wingless along tenement
Windowsills, these public ghosts chant
In harmony with the Angelus

Their metered but hidden drone
Is nature's fixed refrain, concelebrating
The High Mass of Referendum

Alas, their song with its urgent lyrics
Seeps into the night -- some forget it
Even before the Consecration

The little social workers fall from grace
Leaving transparent shells
At the altars of justice

Yet the song returns anew
With each ageless eve
Haunting the Kingdom in full

While life in the tree tops
Continues without interruption
Gloria In Excelsis Deo!

## *LUCKILY*
## *LIFE GOES ON*

# Circuit Breaker

History Spirals – and
The world ever in process
Coils back upon itself

With a swerving arc that repeats
Pirouetting upward, Learning
From its own rotation

That the surface of things
Changes but the center remains
A fixed energy

The Spiraling world ascends
Through a mysterious universe
Dragging change along

And audaciously
It unfurls itself
In virulent synapse

Momentous -- churning
A Paragon of Revolution
As a new Chapter begins

## IT'S GOOD TO STIR THE POT

# China Doll Take Two

A few pages back
You sat with me
On the cold enamel paint
Of a wooden shelf
As I held on tight
Dangling my legs from the shelf
Stay with me now
Inside this porcelain poem
Of pinafore and lace
And feel the disconnect,
As we both dangle our legs from the shelf
Look around this shadow-box world
With your own antiseptic eyes
Your own anxious and gnarled attitude
That's what this book is about -- you
They say you can't know a person
Until you've walked in his or her shoes
Or stiffened up from the same
Kind of terror as the other poor devil
Hang in there and you'll get the
Feeling back in your legs
I won't force you through
The pain of being knocked over
Of bleeding from the fear in your brain
I will ask one thing of you though
I will ask you to try to understand
That feeling hollow isn't fun
Sounding hollow isn't exciting
So understand that change must
Happen to make sense out of things
If you don't get this, you won't find
Your new rhythm
Your thoughts won't leap
Outside your head
And your spirit won't reform
I simply ask you to…edit

# *I Need To Edit My Spirit Now And Then*

# Birds of Pray

The sun was going down but not without a fight.
The struggle left the sky bruised in shades of purple,
yellow and blood-shot pink.  It was violently beautiful.

Cutting the color above the horizon like capillaries were
two lines.  One line high up held the Black Birds of
November.  One lower down held the week's wash.
The black birds swayed in and out of the bruised background
discussing the process of stringing lines.  They liked the
lines.

Lines gave them vantage to discuss all the other processes
that needed deliberation.  With such a dramatic setting
one would think that birds would be discussing high-
minded topics, philosophical and rare.  But the talk turned
to clotheslines, then to the small clothes hanging on the lines.

It was conceded that their own very small appearance against
The majestic labyrinth sky meant that they were somewhat
insignificant.  What's a bird to think of something with such
small proportion as itself?

But one bird, a bird of inconspicuous wit and wisdom said,
"If someone out there was looking at us strung high above the
clothes, we would appear smaller than the clothes, yet we are
made of feather and blood.  They are but cotton."  This thought
stunned the other birds and they stopped swaying.

"The first shall be last," said the inconspicuous bird, "and the
seemingly small and insignificant shall endure long after the
setting sun. When the lines are cut and the clothes are taken
down, the birds will usher in the morning light.   They will remain
because they ponder a line of thought that leads to the value of
small wonders, like the consequence of marred horizons.  They will
abide like the lilies."

And after a time the clothesline fell away, and the horizon fell
away but the birds, they chose to stay.

## *FROM MY VANTAGE POINT I SEE...*

# Metered Drafting

Creation is Everlasting
Nothing much else is --
Each day we pursue
The truth in our own
Sounds  -- What sounds
Right to us...Holding on
Determined to provide
Accurate rhythms
As we proceed
Often without confidence
Through the fast flying
Universe of words --
Plucking truths
Composing Fabrications
And Fictions --
We try to force what might be
Into what is

# WHAT SOUNDS RIGHT
## TO ME

# A Lifetime Vigil in Amherst

She was a litany
Aspiring in a process
Called prayer --
She never wrote a word
Without a challenge from nature
To compare its precision
With her description --
She dared society
To find a shallow center
In her rhyme --
She dared the pious
To find God in nature
Making the ordinary sublime --
Her literary liturgy
Consecrated words
Into psalms of piety --
So sensitive was she
That bobolinks
Were sacred society --
In merry melancholy
She offered obscurity
As her sign of peace --
Postulant, whose prayer
Is nature's sanctity
Ora Pro Nobis

## PIOUS OR POMPOUS...ME?

## Perhaps An Epitaph

If my words do not die with me

They might be meant for someone else

Someone who is trying to climb out

Of old connections that were

Made in other lifetimes

For them my words will be new

Certainly that's why I read poetry

If my words survive my death

They must contain the spirit

Of all the survivors who climb

In and out of books regularly

Till they reach new life times

My words might be for them

If they don't die with me

# *CAN I LEAVE A LEGACY OF WORDS?*

_____
_____
_____
_____
_____
_____
_____
_____
_____
_____
_____
_____
_____
_____
_____
_____
_____
_____
_____
_____
_____
_____
_____
_____

# The Hands of Time

Most really smart people

Advise not to use clichés

Personally, I can't get

Enough of them

They are condensed speech

Allspice for sentences

And they're packed with meaning

In a fast-paced society

They should regain

The respect they deserve


Of course, Enough is Enough

# I WISH SOCIETY WAS...

# From Dust Thou Art

From the event horizon
The stars catapult
Toward outer limits
Ejecting from the
Lap of a solar
Powered slingshot --
Then hurtling through
An unfamiliar space
They explode and
All at once the
Universe is lit by
Raucous stardust --
It rushes down
Sticking like glitter
On the Eyelashes
Of my mind's eye --
In glittering darkness
I fly to the surface
Of my imagination
To watch the
Birth of wonder
To anticipate my
Newest notion
From the stars

# I GET MY IDEAS FROM

_____

_____

_____

_____

_____

_____

_____

_____

_____

_____

_____

_____

_____

_____

_____

_____

_____

_____

_____

_____

_____

_____

_____

_____

_____

_____

_____

# Glorious Decisions

The Morning Glory
Cuts a figure—Randomly
Through Unfamiliar Territory

      She heads for Freedom
      From her Vine
      Then does an About Face

In Double take the
Glory Scout ponders
A young girl's station

      She'd like to bolt
      Forever, but it would
      Ruin her Reputation

She spirals up
And round the post
Until she's quite secure

      A model sentry
      Guarding entry
      Steadfast and Demure

# *I LOVE MY VINE*

# Goldie Locks

Sheaf of Wheat

Her hair unparted

Bows to trees and

Cascading leaves

Little Lady Landscape

Just getting started


Winds comb through

For one last look

Her tresses thrashed

Then discretely stashed

First golden curls

Pressed in a book

# *Sweet Memories*

# The Vineyard

Behind the leaves
On a spiraling vine
Is a microcosm of life
The Society of Wine
Violets, lavenders, blues
One cluster, many hues

Together for life
Gathered by grace
Reflecting color
Disregarding race
No segregations
Just dignified relations

A lexicon of flavor
Crushed and pressed
In unity of purpose
Completely undressed
In this champagne society
Communion is variety

# I Must Look Up The Word "Oxymoron"

# Gypsy Rainbows

A summer sprinkler
Swings to and fro
Leaving melting
Rainbows nice and low
They fall in the grass
Making sparkling dew
And upon each drop
They're crated anew
With the banging sound of cymbals arcing

The gypsy rainbows
Dance in the air
Then settle in grass
Any old where
They haven't a care
For where they light
They steal away
In the dark of night
With the swishing sound of cymbals arcing

Wanting only a kiss
From your private glance
They dance in the mist
And take a chance
That their little circus
Was seen before
They pulled up stakes
For the lawn next door
With the echoing sound of cymbals arcing

# WHEN DELICACY
## JUST HAPPENS

_____

_____

_____

_____

_____

_____

_____

_____

_____

_____

_____

_____

_____

_____

_____

_____

_____

_____

_____

_____

_____

_____

_____

_____

_____

_____

# Bird Technology

I once said only change is constant
But I was wrong
The birds have shown me otherwise
I first opened my eyes in 1948
Although I don't remember
But I do remember the first
Sounds I ever heard
I guess I was around 7 years old
So it must have been about 1955
That I remember hearing the song
Of the Cardinal in the morning
I looked out the window and
Into a wall of white lacy pear blossoms
There was a red so bright
It took my breath away
That glorious red Cardinal was
Good enough to sing me awake
But how did he know I was there
Ah bird technology, you can't beat it


I've listened to that bird ever since
And as the years ensued
I watched the pear tree die
My childhood home fall down
My hair turn from brown to gray
My youthful days fade away
But that bird song
I first heard back in 1955
That has not changed
It would seem like the end of the world
If it were to change now and
It would seem like the end of the world

If I were to stop loving ED's poetry
Anytime I can refer to her line
"help a fainting robin unto his nest again"
I swoon
It's the greatest image in literature and
The sweetest thing I can imagine
Other than the song of the cardinal


Emily's robin and my cardinal are the
Archangel Birds who fly as escorts
They fly along side of the
Blackbirds who land upon
The electrical lines and power lines
The lines we wouldn't notice
If it wasn't for the black color guard
The company of black birds land and perch
They watch and talk and determine
That the things we've done
Like creating weapons of mass destruction
Like pulling the oil out of the Earth
Then leaking it into the water
They know about these things and
Well, I'm embarrassed to show my face
Around a bird that is
But they are all forgiveness
Just this morning I woke up
To the sound of bird song
From all my conversations with the stars
I now know the birds are magic

The bird I heard this morning
It's the same bird I heard back in 1955
Singing the same song
And that's the hope that

Emily Dickinson wrote about
Hope really is the thing with feathers
The bird song is our signal that before
We can cause destruction from weapons
Or completely poison the water and soil
With the oil we stole from the Earth
Or the nuclear waste we generate
The archangel birds will pray for wisdom
To guide the black birds through what
Could have been the end times
So they are strong enough to peck and peck
To completely peck away the lines
So that we lose power and
Are rendered harmless to ourselves
Ah the technology of birds

# THERE IS ONE THING
# THAT MAKES ME SWOON

_____

_____

_____

_____

_____

_____

_____

_____

_____

_____

_____

_____

_____

_____

_____

_____

_____

_____

_____

_____

_____

_____

_____

_____

_____

_____

_____

# Heart Breaker

In a Pool of Distraction

Passion slips Unnoticed

Under the heart's Pearl Canopy

It cozies in like a Butterfly

Lights in a Garden of Sand

Fluttering the old order away

Into Careless Disarray

Like Sparkling White Waves

Break an Aqua Blue Routine

# *Oh...To Break The Routine*
## *Or*
### *If You Would Like To End With A Poem*
#### *Try Writing an*
##### *"Ode To A Broken Routine"*

# The Offering

If Obscurity is the realm of error
I certainly make a lot of mistakes
For my creations have traveled
Few steps beyond my door
I should be happy with the
Obvious serenity that brings
But poetry is not born to lie
Like shadows 'neath the sun
I can remain obscure but
Verses that proceed from
The chambers of my heart
Should be sung
I'll stand with Emily
In a maiden's white dress
And in gossamer bolts of melody
I'll address *My letter to the World*

*Find my fascicles in dresser drawers*
*Courier them to Houses --*
*Let them shine like stars*
*Lest they be forgotten*

174

*NOW THAT I'VE  SEEN MY WORDS IN PRINT*

*I'M READY TO WRITE*

*MY LETTER TO THE WORLD*

www.ingramcontent.com/pod-product-compliance
Lightning Source LLC
Chambersburg PA
CBHW031957040426
42448CB00006B/401